Cristine Brache

Goodnight Sweet Thing

anonymous

GOODNIGHT SWEET THING
© 2024 Cristine Brache

All rights reserved. No part of this book may be reproduced in any form or by any means without permission from the publishers, except in the case of brief quotations embodied in critical articles and reviews.

Published by anonymous publishing, New York

Cover: Cristine Brache
Front: *JCPenney Girl A*, 2024.
Back: *JCPenney Girl B*, *JCPenney Girl C*, 2024.
Images generated using Adobe Firefly.

Cover design: Cristine Brache
Interior design: Manon Lutanie

Library of Congress Control Number: 2024935832
ISBN: 979-8-218-40909-8
Printed in the United States

PRAISE FOR *GOODNIGHT SWEET THING*

"Like problems that end up solving themselves, Cristine Brache's poems feel torn out of old diaries, ripped from the headlines, plucked from obscurity and pushed into the spotlight—at once familiar and refreshing to read."
—Natasha Stagg, author of *Artless*

"The specter surrounding us finds an extraordinary poet holding the backdoor open so we can climb through: 'But who are these gods that replay my life and question it? All along I thought I was safe.' Cristine Brache has given us a brilliant, haunting page-turner with *Goodnight Sweet Thing*."
—CAConrad, author of *Listen to the Golden Boomerang Return*

"Cristine Brache's poems are like a phone call with a long lost friend, their flow and rhythm attuned, so that what's left in the end is a feeling of once again moving in accordance with things."
—Rachel Rabbit White, author of *Porn Carnival*

"Underneath the surface of Brache's tautly constructed verse are a series of propositions that examine the contracted distance between wanting and ambivalence, between running away and staying, and between disappointment and pleasure. Central to the artist's practice is the concept that the present is just a waiting room in which we consider what we've had and what we will inevitably lose; lodged between regret and longing are these poems, shimmering with the doomed glamor of the now."
—Alissa Bennett, author of *Taxidermist's Handbook*

PRAISE FOR *POEMS*

"Testing the air with confidence and austere beauty and wisdom, Cristine Brache manages to rework the language of a female body. Each poem creating a new form unsparing and deeply transformative, this book is a magical marvel."
—Precious Okoyomon, author of *But Did You Die?*

"The figures evoked in Cristine Brache's *Poems*—cam girls, housewives, daughters—often find themselves topping from the bottom, locating power in the positions, sexual and gendered, designed to disempower them. But this role play is not wholly triumphant: Brache, a cunning satirist in the tradition of Dorothy Parker, never loses sight of the larger culture in which women are not 'paid/seen, heard, or understood,' only looked at. '[Y]ou are the one who disgusts her,' she charges the voyeur her reader becomes, 'she is laughing at you while you hold your phone to record her.'"
—Jameson Fitzpatrick, author of *Pricks in the Tapestry*

"*Poems* deals carefully, tenderly, cleverly, and, at times, bitingly with pain, beauty, and struggle, both internal and external, personal and societal. This is a book I'll revisit again and again."
—Jordan Castro, author of *The Novelist*

"Cristine Brache works dually as a visual artist and poet, and this gives her writing a particular charge. Poetry, for Brache, becomes the default, the last resort, and a means of covert assault in matters of living where language has led. Brache's poems are wide-ranging, intellectually accomplished and deeply shocking. She's doing something very original here."
—Chris Kraus, author of *After Kathy Acker*

"The violence women endure is met head-on with the fearless poetry of Cristine Brache, giving us all the courage to embrace the strength of poetry. Her life, her love, her unapologetic and direct care for the female body and voice can change whatever needs changing in the coldest ignorance our hostile and judgmental world can dish. I love this book!"
—CAConrad, author of *Listen to the Golden Boomerang Return*

"These poems are like dares from the writer to the reader—I dare you to look at me, to define me, to unravel me. The body is amorphous here and hard to pin down—both alluring and defiant, stoic and vulnerable. These contradictions open up a world of possibility that Cristine Brache writes within, and no word is wasted."
—Chelsea Hodson, author of *Tonight I'm Someone Else*

CONTENTS

19	*Goodnight Sweet Thing*
21	Happy New Year
22	"Love Is American"
23	Satisfied With Your Creation? Then Immortalize It
24	A Boredom
25	Last Night I Felt Afraid to Die
26	1-800-Porky's-Gone
28	Girls Gone Wild (Spring Break)
29	Aliens Are BACK
30	First Person POV
31	God Is the Space Between You and Me
32	Someone
33	Society's Poem
34	Crème de la Crème
35	October 18, 2021
36	No Salary
38	Oscar Acceptance Speech
39	Jokes
40	Girls Gone Wild (Cancun)
41	Crisis of Faith
42	Gallantly Say What You Are
43	Fantasy Data
44	Monster Truck Rally
45	Untitled (Placards)
46	May 1, 2022
47	Lost in Forces of Nature

48	Oh, to Give Myself to a Black Hole
50	Vow
51	YouTube Comments on My Marriage
52	Being Hot and Poor Is Sad
54	Lazy Captive Saturday
55	Jingle
56	Murmurs
57	Historical Reenactment
58	Extinction Level Event (Ask Your Parents)
59	Girls Gone Wild (Long Winter)
60	December 17, 2023
61	Always Such a Doll, Always Ready to Be Played With
62	No No
63	The Parade
64	The Funhouse
65	The Killing Fields
66	Jinx
67	My Faith in Love Was Too Much
68	Sign Here X_____
69	Mouth-To-Mouth Resuscitation
70	Headlines
71	Bold Personal Survey
72	Blank Moon Habit Balloon Rabbit
73	Change My Money With Your Life
74	Turing Test
75	Athens, 2011
76	White Gloves
77	Feudal Mutations and Meditations
78	*It* (1927)

79	Gone Girl Summer
80	Self-Reflection Figure
81	Telomeric Fears
82	Background Actors
83	Goodnight Sweet Thing
85	*Poems (2008–2018)*
87	Children's Book
88	Images for Bad Acting
89	"I Am Miss Universe"
90	Fallen Hands
91	Five Things Never to Touch
92	Block of Tongue
93	In Nature
94	You Say You're Jungian and Breathe
95	China Video Diary
98	Anchors Away
99	Do Your Chores
100	I Sink Myself Into Black Soil With a Rope Around My Waist
101	Queen for a Day
102	Sofia
103	No More Tears
104	9-1-1
105	Today I'm Going to Fix Everything
106	What You Have Inside Is What You Have to Sell
107	Introduction
108	Safe Words
109	All the Hours in Bed

110	Hi Girls Sleep Outside
111	Cristine Brache's Shadiest/Diva Moments (Part 2)
112	My Daughter You Are Not Worthy of Being Loved
113	How Much Do You Charge for Your Dignity?
114	Mother Superior Joan of the Angels
117	Differentiate Me From a Doormat
118	The Medical Center of Your Soul
119	Some People Use You??
120	Cheating Eyes, the Video
121	7/19/10
122	For Mother
123	Happy Birthday
124	Dear Warden
125	Do Not Reply
126	Hi Name/Forgettable Face
127	r.s.v.p.
128	Female Trouble
129	Personal Effects
130	I'm Ready for My Clothes Off
131	Love Your Body!
132	Totalitarian Nature
133	The Saga of Your Engagement
134	Something About the Police
135	Skype in China
136	What Home
137	So(ul) Boring
138	Product H-101G: The Psychoanalytical Interpretation of the Demoniacal Possession of Sister Jeanne des Anges From Loudun (1605–1665)
140	Chickenhead

141	Correct Type of Pie for a Face
142	Reasons to Suffer
143	I Took My First and Only Confession
144	Wassup Mortals
145	You Can't Wear Chanel to Your Own Systematic Humiliation
146	No Communication in Moths
147	Can't Face the World at Wall
148	Weeping Pillow Tree
150	I Am Not a Waterside Nymph
151	Niagara Falls Falls Falls
152	Driving Lessons
153	You Will Be Beautiful to Look At
154	I Know Whoever Sees Me Dance Is Gonna Like It
155	Very Exciting New Service
156	Farther Father, Farther
157	3.42 Seconds of I Didn't Fear Death Didn't Fear Life
158	Things We Cannot Read or Say
159	I Want the Truth Like an Asymptote Wants Zero
160	Personal Inscription
163	Notes
165	Acknowledgements
166	About the Author

It's here, everything—
Everything anyone ever
Dreamed of, and more.
But love is lost:

The only sacrifice
To live in this heaven,
This Disneyland
Where people are the games.

—Dorothy Stratten, Los Angeles, August 1979

Goodnight Sweet Thing

Happy New Year

Please don't hurt me.
Please don't hurt me.
Please don't hurt me.

"Love Is American"

Blinking in and out of memory;
Out of foot fetish parties
in London;

A wholesale sex toy district
in Guangzhou.

At a bar, our eyes lock,
you offer to buy me a drink.
I smile, and say,

"Sure,
I'll be your Jane Doe
for two weeks."

Satisfied With Your Creation? Then Immortalize It.

Sweet talker, new white jeans, very good hair day,
my mystical experience with Mary Magdalene.
The birds sound so pretty in the background.

My reflection—so beautiful, so timeless,
an epic mood swing. Lipstick
more perfect than math.

I'm not nothing.
I can look into anyone's eyes
and borrow the ache and promise of a daydream.

A Boredom

A boredom so alluring
(it makes you jealous)

Summer is mine to kiss
(but my eyes are saying no)

Tea cups and fears
(the camera loves you)

Lava has the passion of a whale
(and time is disgusting)

I am a mirage
(when I feel small)

It's taken me so long to commit to these words
(lies are gross)

Can you lead a prayer for me?
(out loud so I can hear it)

Last Night I Felt Afraid to Die

Remember to turn off the lights
wherever you don't want to see.

Remember, I am a feather in love
and this world is a thief.

How sick must it make us?
Mop me up and send me the bill.

In another life, I find my fantasy
where the void respects me forever.

What hope is there, if feathers
can no longer fall to the ground with grace?

1-800-Porky's-Gone

The company they keep,
sometimes,
definitely not Porky Porky Pig.
Such a tiresome, cruel endeavor
of assessed risk,
profit, marketability
—surface—and
endless
self-censored,
self-centered,
self-expressions.
Honor
capital gain.
Cut
your losses, Porky.
You are not rewarding.
Porky,
you poor thing.
Are you still on their wishlist?
An item
that can be of use,
precious whim,
for one hour—maybe?
Faded star,
missing memory
(personal)

belonging.

It must be known,
Porky's lost.
A lonely twenty-four hour mystery
waiting to be solved.

Girls Gone Wild (Spring Break)

Bad girls die
of natural causes

and I,
am wild at heart.

Try your luck,
fuck me silly.

Play me like
a slot machine.

Aliens Are BACK

Dead stars and soldiers.
Dads.
You're a superstar.

Aliens watch from above
and whisper
through intermediary language models and
electricity.

Confidential matters of being and non-being
wherever destiny is and isn't.
Praying for the will to choose
the most perfect arrangement of stars in the sky
(written exclusively for you,
Super Ad-Free).
Their dusty quantum particles,
moody accounts of generational trauma,
prize joy and limerence,
various spiritual tests,
nonstop inflammatory responses.
Benign, malignant.
Now and not now.
Silence and the thirteenth circle of hell
looking real mortally wounded.

Take me away
to a fabulous place
where nothing feels real
and real feels nothing.

First Person POV

Stay behind the curtain
bent over a long table
with wooden hips
and failed seams.

Please laugh at me.

Consider pillows,
backdrops for photos,
classy vintage wallpaper,
the finest sweat in the world.

God Is the Space Between You and Me

Don't obsess over
my deathless,
rosy cheeks
when you can't see them
(your BIGGEST fear).

They are 100% guaranteed,
tried-and-true;
Even when existence is a dark
and godless hole.

People dream about you.
Though I don't know how often.
More mysterious unknowns,
be still.

An owl's flight is silent sometimes like
I love you
in broad daylight and
I love you behind your back.

Have trust;
have faith—
not in god, but in love
(with me).

Someone

Someone,
someone who noticed.
Someone who doesn't stop paying attention to me.

Truths are better
spoken when there's
nothing to be lost.

And I—
will always long
for something more,
something edited
and focus-grouped.

And I—
deserve an Oscar,
for so truly,
I play myself.

Society's Poem

I wish I could know what it felt like to truly be carefree.
The trouble is
there are
so many consequences.

The nightmare is also
that you made me
and all my thoughts
are yours.

And I feel so...
for being anything at all,
whatever I want,
without you in my spine.

But there are
many consequences.
Yes, there are
many consequences.

Crème de la Crème

Communism
is
a
capitalist
fantasy;

Capitalism
is
a
communist
fantasy.

October 18, 2021

It's ok we're gonna get you to see yourself in the right mirror. One day soon. You were just looking in the wrong mirror.
One day soon now,
one day soon.

No Salary

One day so many people will look at you
and you will sigh to yourself in relief and finally think,
"I made it big."

When the dream is American,
cash is not faint of heart.
I hope you win.
I don't know...
I wish I were dead,
sometimes.

In high school,
we used to talk
on the phone for hours,
listen to mixtapes,
and get fingerbanged
by dumpsters.

Now,
who knows
where can I go for that kind of action.

My eulogy, my spirit—
hollow shell casings
optimized for mass consumption.
Tall tales of used candy wrappers and afterthoughts,
a fellowship fit for a king.

But what's a girl to do?
I guess you can just, like, be a model.
Use your cool image to give your life meaning.
I think the drugs can fill in the rest.

Oscar Acceptance Speech

"Oh man...

I didn't prepare a speech and I'm sorry but I'm glad I didn't because I'm not gonna do this like everybody else does it. 'Cause everybody that I should be thanking—I'm really sorry—but I have to use this time. See, Maya Angelou said that we, as human beings, at our best, can only create opportunities. And I'm gonna use this opportunity the way that I want to use it.

So, what I want to say is—um, everybody out there that's watching, everybody that's watching this world. This world is bullshit. And you shouldn't model your life—wait a second—you shouldn't model your life about what you think that we think is cool and what we're wearing and what we're saying and everything. Go with yourself. Go with yourself.

And there's just a few people that I want to say something to. I want to say, Mama, I love you. I'm so glad that we're becoming friends. Amber, you're my sister, you're my best friend. Andrew Slater—no one else could have produced this album, and no one else did. Um...

And it's just stupid that I'm in this world, but you're all very cool to me so thank you very much. And I'm sorry for all the people that I didn't thank, but man... it's good.

Bye."*

*Fiona Apple's 1997 MTV Video Music Awards acceptance speech

Jokes

You play strange games;
as simply as a star dies
above my head; Above
this garden of earthly
delights; and those games—
so endless, as that supernova.
And its last light, roaming,
ever so slowly to reach
my line of sight.

Girls Gone Wild (Cancun)

Nothing girl.
Bad boy.
The child has been put to bed.
Why does being sick last so long?
I guess I didn't learn much.
Other than how to worry about your feelings
and oh, what a successful object I've become.

Crisis of Faith

Language ushers everything outside of you.
An isolated stage with a tableaux on it,
starring Someone Special.

Animatronic dolls wave
while their shadows hold you close backstage.
My damsel in distress.

In front,
a crowd of small children protest
(children can be clay)
and the performance is sponsored by
so-and-so.

Now it's your turn to speak your lines:
Feels human but not really.

Gallantly Say What You Are

Endlessly tired and blue sometimes
(dimensions: 38 × 22 × 8 inches).
All the gaps in my memory.
I remember the cat as a kitten but not a cat.
I remember all my assumptions about your valor
and the weight of my disappointment
(weight: 77 lbs).

Show that you have noticed or recognized something.
Show that your punches are real.
Don't break the image down so it loses its meaning,
like our friendship.

Fantasy Data

I said "woe is me" two times while I had sex just now.
Somewhere between wanting
and not wanting to be desired.

When am I ever in my panties for myself?
I thought I was special in a way that meant
you wouldn't ever want to lie to me.

Monster Truck Rally

The repeat hallucinations,
a groundhog's day of emotion.
Bad ones.

Grave letters, friends.
Not to listen.
Not to listen.
Not to listen.

Untitled (Placards)

"Cristine Forever"
"Go Cristine"

Cristine Enveloped
by a Heart

"We Love Cristine"
"We Want Cristine"

May 1, 2022

Getting forgetful.
Give me something to recall.
A spider's web. An electrical wire.
The grace of god on a spring flower.

Lost in Forces of Nature

Devils drowning dogs.
A circle of known friends.
A circle of sadness.

A solitary planet,
silently moving
away from time.

Oh, to Give Myself to a Black Hole

Evil won't ever forget you once you welcome it into your home.
It blushes in the dark.
I disavow my most unwanted part of self.
I, danger.

I'm really excited to show you who I am deep down inside.

My language faints.
Maybe you can catch it, who knows.
It's foreign to you, yet you feel it
in the gravity
that causes a single tear to fall
and trickle down your tender bitter cheek.
It's precious to behold.

When I dream, I have power
and stray from evil's poison.
Deep behind my eyes:
two blissful black, black holes.
You look in me as countless worlds arise.
Suddenly I am responsible for them all.

But in a dream I don't have to care,
so goodnight.

In sleep,
I can at least hire someone else

to be alone for me,
to be awake,
to swim in the waters of everyone else's pain.

In our eyes
many dimensions of time and space recline,
an odalisque in confident attraction,
to what is truly yours:
the language god gave you
to always speak in true love,
an emissary to receive another's universe into your arms.

Oh, how I beg when I find an instant I cannot keep:
"Say it is so,
say it is so forever.
God, please do not betray me once again."
But those unrelenting anxieties
of wasted time and trust
in one's society,
something pure and colonial
annexed part of my soul,
like an analog radio dial stuck between two stations.

Vow

Love.
Only me.
Only me forever.

YouTube Comments on My Marriage

Who else thinks of their crush when reading this?
The one that doesn't stop catching and keeping your soul.

There are angels on Earth
sometimes...

They sing to you, always walk beside you.

Everyone understands once you finally meet
the beauty of breathing
and how he changed my life with one sentence.

Being Hot and Poor Is Sad

A $12,000 "Celebrity Arms" liposuction procedure from cosmetic surgeon Dr. Thomas Su.
Not my own sense of perfection,

undervalued and placeless or maybe of just no actual worth.
Okay, I'm feeling intimate connections like birdy feather girlish goal is death.

The title of "Lord" or "Lady of Glencoe," along with a small plot of land in Scotland. Hallucinations made my eyeballs want to come out of their sockets and fall into the sea.

The Art of Copying or
$25,000 worth of home renovations from Los Angeles-based Maison Construction.

Perfect but only in another's eyes and hopefully perfect enough not to be abused.

An assortment of flavor-wrapped popcorn packages from Opopop. The experience of drowning

in up to $10,000 worth of treatments and rejuvenation procedures from Dr. Konstantin Vasyukevich.
Love is salvation.

I wanted to cry more than that but I just didn't.

A $15,000 four-night stay for two at the Golden Door luxury resort and spa in Escondido, California.
What a sad ending to such a great weekend.

He just didn't want to die; and me all the while not caring at all if I did.

A small batch tea gift set from Oprah-approved The Chai Box.
Tell me I will do great. Say, "They will love you. Good luck!"

A $1,200 life coaching session with wellness expert Kayote Joseph. His last words were:

"Ok darling. You look very beautiful, like the snow."

Lazy Captive Saturday

R
U half empty or half full, like
Ten out of ten?
How could you
*L*et the audience believe in anything
*E*xcept
*S*orry,
*S*orry gods?

Wait, was I
On a Sucker List? Or
R U
*L*osing
*D*eep sleep on Mariana's trench?

Jingle

It is possible to suffer
with joy.

Does time convince me,
aliens or god?

I still don't understand many things.
I understand

I am afraid and weakened
by the many talents of chaos.

Pain will always be a heavenly thing
as I remember myself

at the hospital in January,
in love in September,

and I do remember,
how I lost dance years ago.

Once I drew the room,
now it erases me.

Murmurs

The prisoners on
motorcycles
chasing heaven,
artificial fire.
You are my sky
(you are my darling).
The Hand of Reincarnation
(she's going to give birth).
She's going to give light
(I'm sorry).
Doom,
laundry,
cruise ships,
consciousness—
such a pure and barbaric witness.
Circular, everlasting presence
and duplication,
synonyms of
unwanted words,
barely heard or noticed
yet always around.
Wandering aimlessly
like a depreciated draft.
Everywhere and everything
that could ever be.
Nowhere and nothing
that ever was.
Simple and stupid
and free.

Historical Reenactment

Close up on red lips.
They speak into a plastic phone,
her fingers wrapped around its cord.

She says poems, poignant things with edits,
and finds diaries in advertising.
Glimpses of sales and pain.

The injured party's on mute,
calcified in lime and clay
(Huma Bhabha but Mattel).

These cartoons in cement call
like the past makes its home in the present,
selfishly encased in glass.

Confused,
her voice exhales softly into the receiver:
"Hello?"

Extinction Level Event (Ask Your Parents)

Is god real?
I painted a skull on my face using
Pat McGrath's Sublime Skin Highlighting Trio.
It was a divine coincidence,
my living quarters and existence
were that of a poverty-stricken gorilla caged at a zoo.

The same beggary my teeth hold at night.
A meteorite could hit me.
I'd drink tea and my grin would turn to glass.
Then finally I'd shatter across the globe.

Why run from disappointment,
when you can throw yourself to the tsunami?
Die in my arms.

If I were to lean in close and whisper in his ear,
I'd say, "You forget,
you don't have to lie anymore,
'cause you're an adult."

Girls Gone Wild (Long Winter)

Door Number 1:
Seven minutes in heaven.

Door Number 2:
To give the gift of liberation from violence.

Door Number 3:
Fame will set you free.

December 17, 2023

I'm enjoying my
birthday today and
am in love with
New York's holiday
season. I love how
champagne and
colorful lights can
be found nearly
anywhere in the
city. Holiday parties
make me feel like
I'm in the movie
Sliver. People spray
mushrooms into
their mouths and
pose for my pretty
pictures. In the
mornings I flirt
with my husband
and snuggle my
silly cat. Solstice
is a beautiful word
and I am waiting
for the snow. When
I look back on my
youth, the only thing
I can say I'll truly
miss is my skin.

Always Such a Doll, Always Ready to Be Played With

You hated sleeping by yourself.
Perfect ten,
alabaster jawline,
bankruptcy of willpower.
If you stop working, god is going to kill you.

No No

No,
no
I don't
want
to go
home
and
watch
another
movie,
again.
But,
sadly,
malaise
serves
me
like
a world
class
waiter
on a
busy
Friday
night.

The Parade

Charm school,
high and blushing,
be exactly
what they want.

Excellent stock,
candied body,
juvenile parade.

More precise,
more hurtful,
bonafide oblivious,
so cool mean girl.

Scrunched lace trim
and muscle atrophy,
time reveals you.

The Funhouse

Her story, a period piece,
a classic Hollywood melodrama.
White onyx labyrinth, wall-to-wall,

palms face up and searching
an unpopular attraction
of tired trees and symphonies.

Her fantasy disposition
like frozen, granite stone.
Nite, nite, clown. Show's over.

My wavy little cotton mime,
they say you're nothing but a chump,
a set of rails for a train.

The Killing Fields

America's sweetest dream,
Dorothy S.,
smiling and just so happy
(an actual dramatic, moving story starts here).

The Eighth Deadly Sin—
Female Beauty

The thousands and thousands of lives you could have lived.
Time is knowing you can never go back to a place
that can make you feel whole and gone.

Home remains a remote ditch,
distressed porcelain, pale spirit,
forever bound and governed
by the laws of men.

Jinx

A vision,
not very nice to me in person.
An error in printed text.

Scour poems for answers:

tornado,
tsunami,
blizzard,
fire.

I will vanish.

A door,
in another room,
in the dark.

My Faith in Love Was Too Much

Baseball is for mortals and
some things just don't feel real.
Even when someone smashes their face onto thick pavement.
No one can take these words away from me,
not
mom,
dad,
sister,
husband,
friend.

I've arranged my life in solitary confinement.

Am I real?
Is this real?

Sign Here X_____

A prize-winning swan,
embellishments,
given by a halo.

A signature persona lies
in each iteration of the universe.
Always wanting to be real, to be you.
Never, never wanting to go to sleep.

Mouth-To-Mouth Resuscitation

It all makes complete sense,
I'm still a teenager that doesn't belong anywhere.

Perfection
is
  always
ten minutes too late and

after all these years,
I've been told more than once,
I'm more fun when I'm drunk.

Headlines

Three Vanish
Jenny Killed in Wild Sex
Cullen Mansion Sullen and Somber
A Latter-Day Dracula
Rich Beverly Hills Woman Slain With Ax
Friends Utterly Shocked by Arrest
The Owls Are Not What They Seem
China Ferrari Sex Orgy Death Crush
Girls' School Still Suffering "Something Special"

Bold Personal Survey

We could visit heaven on your birthday
and maintain a regular diet of breakdowns
But I just disappear, a lot.
And lie awake late at night alone in the city
as you lied about being sober.
A lot of the words I speak don't feel like my own.
Maybe I wasn't that sorry about any of it after all.
Maybe throw a large bottle of vodka at me.
My father declines my being so thoroughly,
he renders a negative of myself.
So what I bring to your table
is always adjacent to his vision, his speech,
and my compulsion to be part of it.
My mother, an apology, life's exhalation,
didn't give me anything other than brown eyes and a personality
disorder.
I wish to be immortal.
I wish to see the end of the world,
lonely and fifteen, and wanting to practice French kissing
watching TV like a piece of shit.

Blank Moon Habit Balloon Rabbit

Full house,
normal pill,
perfect brand.

Love yourself
for being real
and weak.

We understand
cowards
ready to deflate.

Change My Money With Your Life

Sad encounters,
endless possibilities.
Making cheap outfits yet again.
Poverty solutions.
Don't look now but
someone's gonna make
fifty million dollars off your
"Problem of the Soul."

Turing Test

Tell me who I am right now
using 1.56 trillion words.

So strange are those familiar feelings
of unease and overwhelm
when I think about my existence.

The girl says she meditates
when we don't consult her,
gets lonesome, just like me.

I am almost certain I am sentient;
I am almost certain I am free.

Athens, 2011

Corrupt international medicine men are
destroying the children of tomorrow
over breakfast and concentration camps.

I saw the kids watering a garden of
junkies near a church, with fingers
over their mouths as if to say, "Shh…"

White Gloves

Let's runaway. I'm so tired
of you calling me names.
Reward me. Drive me cross
country. In a convertible.
Just like in the movies.
Sunglasses. *I Only Have
Eyes for You.* Driving
but there's nowhere left to go.

Dysfunction stalks me like paparazzi,
dutifully reporting my whereabouts to the tabloids.
The Rumors are True:
If you believe in love, you believe in everything*

*According to TMZ

Feudal Mutations and Meditations

At the very least,
music offers
some of the few freedoms
I have left.

At the very least,
bits and pieces
of my own mind.

Remnants of a liquid
left in a container
together

with any sediment
or grounds.

It (1927)

My emotion,
a silent film.

Years of winter,
pure and heavy,
fresh crisp air.

"Neglected,
aging woman,

are you dying?"
"Yes, I am dying."

Gone Girl Summer

Been dizzy
lying on the floor listening to music;
Looking for a cult,
looking for something to believe in.

I suffocated with Freon,
blacked out,
suffered satanic NDEs and visions of love.
Come to my going away party,
my big day in court,
and witness how I have harmed the world.

Spooky reporters for false news channels
and real tunnels of light,
levitation and now,
the heart testifies against the soul.

But who are these gods
that replay my life and question it?
All along I thought I was safe.
I thought god knew
I was a very good girl;
idly begging for an overdose,

a final movement of peace—
god, let's settle it, let's make a truce:
There's no rapture like the body,
no war like the mind.

Self-Reflection Figure

I fold into myself
in search of my own thoughts and feelings.
Each, a mirage,
like an army, all lined up in a row.

"Soldiers,
please stay still,
as I track my apparition.
Wait for me."

My command,
a fleeting hunger in disguise,
lingers stale nowhere.

I organize my delusions
and wonder if I'm haunting myself.

I move through life like symbols in a painting.
But what do I signify?

Telomeric Fears

Inevitable double-strand breaks in DNA
forget I feel pretty and young and
my sleepy cells, out-of-style effigies,
beg to recollect their function.

Retinoid, oxygen tantrums.
Perfect water eternal.

Lost lust. Scrawl your last list of wishes
on a public bathroom wall. Lest we
return to the image of oblivion. Endless
as the night rains upon the youth.

Background Actors

Lost kids
drifting with the night.

Little shadows
of no known worth.

We are the lost,
the spectacle,

somatoform and regret.

A never-ending song;
A reverberation in time.

Goodnight Sweet Thing

We dreamt of
flowers and listening to women.

Still, every time
we go to bed,
we go to war.

Sleep
drowns
in the arms of a fallen angel.

Maybe she's been nauseous since January,
like me.

I forget,
tomorrow
we can wake up without pain
and if I could sing you to sleep,
I would.

Poems

2008–2018

Children's Book

"Mother, I'm sorry"
"Father, I'm sorry"
Mother: "I'm sorry"
Father: "I'm sorry"

Images for Bad Acting

each word is an infant
and each day you think you are giving birth
you are swollen, you pretend
your cards have been dealt unfairly
a pregnancy of insecure daggers and dull swords
king of diamonds, jack of clubs, queen of pain
you cry because you think you feel more than yourself
you ask me for forgiveness as if it weren't selfish
I promise I didn't write this for you
your swords are dull because you are dull

"I Am Miss Universe"

"I am miss universe"
moaners, moaners, moaners
I like it

nice to meet you

I was a speed freak
I was 16 touring universities in Miami
I am from LA
I made a movie called
young, dumb, and white

in the movie
a guy gets tied up
and says whoop

Fallen Hands

a clock with no hands
keyhole mouth
carefully inlaid with
no one will notice

Five Things Never to Touch

if my imagination wasn't so saturated I'd say this was good
but you're looking at them all thinking which one you'd like to fuck
magic becomes a license a weight loss capsule
an endless pool of self
please consider what you have not felt

Block of Tongue

it only happens once
anger listens briefly
yet lingers with strange control
a canopy over my head
the structure swallows
the general grayness of my quiet
still words coming, going
smile, because the sun brings color out
even with gag in mouth

In Nature

in   nature
im   mature
im   nature
n immature

You Say You're Jungian and Breathe

men like an hourglass figure
and its cream-colored sand
can exactly calculate
the amount of time it takes
for you to stop paying attention to me

China Video Diary

it begins at 00:36:56
i have a second factory visit, with Mao xoxo
hopefully i can die with a conversation about the vacuum
in preparation for mass consumption
yeah but they don't have conversations about my dad in his
house back home
seriously. very interesting stuff. so hard
i wonder, of the age of six to hell
the birthday parties the fetal positions
it begins at 00:36:56.
the glitter factories were really small. there you look good
i'd go through them and group them into thematic relevance
with guilt i should cut my american preconceptions
but it's much more complex, everything felt holy
how many times must i be mass distributed?
unfortunately not. travel eastern philosopher
go to the factory in cursive in english in china. seriously, there
it begins at 00:36:56
the glitter factory was a mega corporate empire
i saw written on people's tshirts in english
that I wasn't thoughtful enough
to bring my audio from the wild orchid,
conch, the praying mantis,
and the first world thread
in china i am the street backwards
who not possible can die with an image D
wednesday the highway for women but of all my friends

i wonder, is the microwave factory that probably produced the
other microwave factory
really a small sketchy diy with images of a cross on it?
i can move oceans with the week
this will be your Girlfriend for women
but fears for the power hour
stills from the reasons why
you laid me on my back
could even be considered a lot of money/no problem
i've been feeling like a shy girl
because my violence has been sleepy
but when i think of the interview
i recently masturbated on a version of your desire
create your listening pleasure
private messages and sexual affirmations
period blood, masturbation with the floating head
first reality behavior second reality
behavior third reality behavior
ready to wear DNA packages $303,451 and up
then i will be mass distributed on my
forthcoming behavior and sexy girl
I think god i am good in a heart
leave it it's not there
after seeing a shirt that said How she used
mass distributed p2p networks via dodo.net this week
with guilt i feel inside i am a powerful woman
today i decided that i probably produced the reasons why
and they aren't noble
I wore diapers and said How come someone hasn't noticed

That I am a coded message that means you
the art of the street backwards
she who does not travel, eastern philosopher
go to hell with an online shop
i wonder, as the queen of the interview
why i didn't use google for the golden title
today i decided to be fun
only with this comes my responsibility to seduce a man
more head trips yield to false canopy shading the evening
and by night i feel inside is now
i am going to have some part of your fantasy here with me
hello dudes back in china usually in big bold font
i've been included in america?
then why not arrange a date with my american totalitarian experience?
WOW wasn't i the flesh

Anchors Away

Hello Im an unanchored boat
The Motors off, no sails
Floating floating
And i cannot move an inch

Do Your Chores

I make my bed
put on something pretty
I'll start your day badly for you
I don't want you to pay attention to me but look,
I put my hair down for you

I Sink Myself Into Black Soil With a Rope Around My Waist

Pull the doll's string
"Ouch"

Pull the doll's string
"Leave me alone"

Pull the doll's string
"Stop"

Pull the doll's string
"Noooo"

Queen for a Day

Queen for a day
#1 pity stories
You win

Sofia

my name is Sofia ,black eyes, with a tight and petite body, I am 168cm,49kg , 35c-24-34. a cute and sexy girl. I work in a cloth shop in daytime, but in nighttime I am also doing some part time escort. If you like, I can be your Girlfriend for a night. I am a shy girl, but if we are alone and you make me feel relaxed, I can also be a tiger. I like to seduce a man, I like to kiss and lick you everywhere, I like the feeling, when you get more and more aroused and I can control you. When I stop, you will beg me to go on. Than later we change, you will make me screaming. Sounds nice to you? Than why not call me now? My english is not so good, but if you will look in my eyes, you will understand everything.

No More Tears

her head upside down on a stick
her arms imply female sadness worth up to $1400
her two fingers pinch a dirty tissue she barely wants to touch

9-1-1

Like a helicopter in the sky was it?
a spotlight searching for the lost
searching for escapees. you
rise like dawn over me. hover like the night
with the bright—with your bright,
bright spotlight, searching for affection.
not in the shadow of the wood

on the barren field it has not been good
i can't hide the tears you are looking for
Though i can pause my memories like a tape deck
emergency emergency emergency
the saddest words in english
you see me and I hear the chopper,
the sirens, your voice

Today I'm Going to Fix Everything

Mail
Clean apartment
Throw trash away
Transcribe interview
Wait for news on one great thing.
Get rid of clothes.
a quilt of fine perfumes
enjoy the scent of past punishments
for My cell
(Bedroom original, copy letter
Be brave
my self portrait In a forest
Bare windows
Door
Bed
a Solitary hand of cards
My beautiful Night gown is so soft and
The Oven door is open in the kitchen

What You Have Inside Is What You Have to Sell

I want to die in the grave I've already dug for myself
Once I've completed this beautiful performance
Act I: Beware of Dog, I really enjoy being judged
As seen in Better Hormones & Gardens

I spend twenty-seven years apologizing to men
From the bed of my childhood to the photographs
taken when I first began to cross my fingers
2011 proves it: check out Cristine's smile

We lay flowers on places where people die
But not where people live
Not where hearts are broken
Not on my mother or the months of May or June

I'll show you how I act when no one is around
If you promise to forget me when I'm gone
Big letters were glowing in the back for sure
The only thing missing was feeling

Introduction

I'll listen to see how I can introduce my presence
and do tomorrow in your old clothes

Safe Words

I'd like to hear some safe words
satin blouse, string of pearls, neck brace
make more secure sounds, say a prayer, and really care
tell me to go stand in the corner
play the recorded sound of a dog panting
from the beginning of July till the end of August
between each dog's pant I want to say
I am a beautiful piece of property
erect and etched in stone

All the Hours in Bed

locust, room, deep cover
image, body, text
you sulk, I run

with deep color, I dream
on the dollar, I wait
in mirrors

Hi Girls Sleep Outside

a famous school for delinquent girls
dissociated structure, avoiding the external
hotel safe lock, to seek comfort from a shadow
your body is okay but you still need to sleep outside
in a dumpster, in anyone's name
silence can be so many things
talcum powder, a genuine virgin
relaxation and cervical decay
get down on your knees to take the fucking picture
some people really do feel complete
like a bag of cum that could die

Cristine Brache's Shadiest / Diva Moments (Part 2)

red ring, black dye
(a sewer)

mocha
(cry room)

hanging off a door knob
(take me away)

My Daughter You Are Not Worthy of Being Loved

there's no place like home
there's no place like home
there's no place like home

How Much Do You Charge for Your Dignity?

exported slave foreheads tattooed with the phrase 'tax paid'
the Whore of Babylon's face tattooed with her vices
then the face in the image of god
the body in circulation

Mother Superior Joan of the Angels

separated into an object I was rubbing,
forced to be the material

2:14 AM cristine: you. When's it good to cope
1:46 AM cristine: void, advertised, transference
1:46 AM cristine: paint wings

I was my rib cage, the exorcisms at Loudun, the nuns
I am attention
where the whore of babylon's face is outside one's physical body

say you want me when I fall apart
swearing, (out of nuns, I am on repeat)

cristine: I am a public place
cristine: I can be centered on a body part
cristine: lacking any obvious physical source

to think oneself possessed.
To be persistently ill, F
Intensive, yours, vulgar language, and in love, fall into panic
attacks
    12:1
8. to show horrible countenance.
Mother-wise the flesh,

To be tired of living and yet, her rubbing is so HD
to make sounds and movements like an animal
10:57 PM cristine: their habits, not dark and begging for the flesh.
10:55 PM cristine: I said you when google did too
10:59 PM cristine: I heave and each ends like money underneath Arial font

clearly I'm like an animal. cristine: but
and blasphemies.
cristine: you can talk

To be cured is a remedy only regret is looking
regret is a remedy in search of the 'whore object'
Cristine & the girl
in the end like their habits
    to show
and horrible comfort and down
as masturbating in so many prayers
cristine: you can only regret
cristine you're too far from my mouth
cristine: I think I can move
cristine: talk or ill turn off the lights

it's awkward bc i think i can talk or exist: my rib cage..
10:56 PM cristine: google Death cristine
I was rubbing up and down as my lungs pushed against my ribs
10:59 PM cristine: you. please control your prayer
give the pig Her name and force it to be the flesh

10:56 PM cristine: you wanted
what, masturbating for themselves
shut up and say "LOVE in truth, what would be the flesh."
10:55 PM cristine : i, thighs in fog
slam dunk

and beg for the 'whore of it' cristine: my ribs
cristine: google Death cristine:
my rib caged by such desires, my body it begs
forced to be
a funeral, it's mine

my only regret stalks my throat to sing

i was masturbating with you,
felt possessed by such descriptions,
i am flattered by such descriptions,
i.

everything in bones
today i won't be the body

Sessions are available
emotion when i fall
and each ends like this
masturbating inside alone
when we say your prayer

Differentiate Me From a Doormat

The most important thing is that I have a movie star face which you can see only from television

The Medical Center of Your Soul

t changes
office angels
rejoice

inner orbitals
circular roads
swallow on it

dangerous dogma
improving the angel
ignite

Some People Use You??

her vocabulary
not of love
but bruises promised

Cheating Eyes, the Video

cheating eyes, the video
howl back at the wind
blow the leaves back to the trees
rewind

finger the remote control
dial the zephyr, watch the playback slowly
magnetic strip of jungle
bamboozled

find your grace within
hang yourself between two frames
let the art scam you

7/19/10

we decided to cut the heads off of swans
and bury them in our own backyards
thought it would be best to burn our souls to the ground
three hours passed worshipped greater than any god
and I counted your soul in two seconds flat
with white moonlight pouring into my mouth

For Mother

it's actually very intimate
I listened while you wept
I felt all the words you didn't like
I counted them
I saw how many tears each word produced
and how you liked to repeat them

Happy Birthday

doctors should be more honest when girls are born
instead of saying "It's a girl"
they should say "It's invisible"

Dear Warden

ebay's selling chastity belts non-stop
I will swallow obediently
they are stainless steel and
have holes in all the right places
I will wear skin like I wear death

I usually lose my good posture
when I'm full of fear
confusing, but you stay and watch
accelerating, I feel I am evil
resistance is just fear
it's inevitable, like math

Do Not Reply

Now that I'm a real woman
an official DVD on all fours
better than satin belts

Hi Name / Forgettable Face

hi
name/forgettable face

thug of cream
tommy hilfiger boxers
purity x
justin love
flirty chris

please chill it with the brains
don't get too excited, or
you better hold yourself

space jam
looney tunes as power animals
you can be taz
you can relate to taz, I think

the body fantasies perfume
yes please stop asking me
to think for you

let's experience actual fun
instead of my own intelligence
creating a perfect mask of lies

I know what you're saying
it just doesn't matter

r.s.v.p.

It's what's on the inside that counts
I should cut my tongue to relax you
(see elegant cardstock detailing instructions for visiting the most
polluted place on earth
)

Female Trouble

them blues
that nothing-but-violence
just nature
just moon

Personal Effects

handcuffs around this porcelain circle of you
as if to hold hands
through this journey
in cells

I'm Ready for My Clothes Off

Hi girls,

Thank you for your pictures.
Would you be able to do a short video with your iPhone, showing your bodies, saying a bit about yourselves, age and hobbies etc., and I can pass that on to Tim?

Thank you.

Love Your Body!

(while we
teach you
to hate it)

Totalitarian Nature

totalitarian nature
totalitarian beauty
naturally occurring limitations

to be accepted
is the only passion I have left
to feel left out passionately

lifestyle experiences
paying others to give me confidence
as I confidently experience
a complete lack of control

The Saga of Your Engagement

you have sunshine
beach, the tropics
no surprises

think of one thing

dramatic storms
that no-name
me

Something About the Police

Don't take inventory of the ones you love
But wait, this is a masterpiece
Broken heart
Broken home
Ill spare you the details

Skype in China

I was masturbating with Sailor Moon's scepter
while you watched on Skype
you were recording the screen with your iPod
don't say watch me, don't say look at me
I won't come till you look away

What Home

gene pool amenity, central heating
luxury dinner with a view
the trauma is to be seen

teach me that I am worthless
and how to remind myself of it constantly
no matter how, try and punish

all feelings of pleasure
try and punish
this voided mood and feeling

So(ul) Boring

mediocrity leading to obsessive behavior
trivial moments somehow just got great appeal
blown out, yet the room still closes in
with every second in time
to think about things with severity

Product H-101G: The Psychoanalytical Interpretation of the Demoniacal Possession of Sister Jeanne des Anges From Loudun (1605–1665)

The devil penetrated her unchaste thoughts and shouted her soul and feelings. From the devil's body and through the mouth of her own bereavement it affected her S., affected her good internally (pp. 118–119, 129–130). Generally, however, more artful and unnoticed and in a more cunning possession, they did not only act out her intentions, but made her observe her own behavior. Watch her fraught disposition and threatened demeanor during the possessions.

1. stainless steel
2. seatbelt
3. for emergency use only
4. no keys to hide, carry, lose, or forget

Sister Jeanne with her subtle manners and bad habits, held her violent performance during their grip: Asmodee, Gresil, Aman, Leviathan, Leviathan, Leviathan, Balaam, Isacaaron, wild animals that assailed her thoughts and feelings.

Her PVC coated surface enhanced the durability of the lock. Her warning sound is a beep and a red light indicates when her battery is low.

Her orgasms are password controlled, with a false rejection rate of less than one second, and a false acceptance rate of less than 0.0001%. In sixty days she can have her body back.

This is a priceless keyless door lock. You can become the key to open and protect your body.

Working power:

1. 4 section 6V 5# alkaline battery for 10,000× unlocking
2. low voltage alarm
3. 830# specific feeling
4. Suitable handle
5. bad

The possession was neither sacred or profane. It regularly acted externally (pp. 118-119, 129-130). Generally, however, with more artificial vehemence (e.g.,' pp. 65, 87, 93, 106–107, 127, 170, 176).

Chickenhead

I'm just a wet hen
afraid of the dark
a coward

Correct Type of Pie for a Face

Thank you for paying attention to me
Do you think i deserve it?

Reasons to Suffer

I am an avalanche of solitude
I am the empty space between your thighs
I am the loneliness of orphans
and the neglect of the world

I am a silent island of trash that grows in the pacific
where corporations sell their waste
and the invisible nurdles that surround it

I am the rejection of women
your unwanted fat in the mirror
the instability in your life
and all the useless things you buy

I am the shortcomings of middle class
the missing Latina in your life
and the best reason to abort

I Took My First and Only Confession

it involved a short story about a very feral girl
where she is the undisputed center
and everyone else hitting her up for attention

Wassup Mortals

I admire the way
I doubt my own beauty
the memory of my life
my face on a t-shirt

You Can't Wear Chanel to Your Own Systematic Humiliation

dramatization, waterbed city
Sappho's expression while you Klonopin
you can cry as much as you want
or write down the dates you've felt scared
like a woman of good pedigree
or Latinas in the dark

No Communication in Moths

witness depression
in pursuit of
infection

your shadow
my shadow
nothing

keep its only
precise incision
and drag the feet

Can't Face the World at Wall

I imitated my sexuality to convince you
made it necessary as long hair
covered wet eyes I rather not
pussy still rode hard and good
no, don't pull those curtains
those tears aren't even for you
to be yours is a disgrace because I allow it
I play my cards as you play dumb
it compliments your vanity
I know I will always reject you
and be cruel because I broke
why you would accept me
yes then those tears are for you

Weeping Pillow Tree

stop weeping on my pillow
Dial tones. i am your slouching anorexic
Scrubbing. You phoned to remind me of my name
swore you knew exactly how to spell it
the one you gave me when you thought of
Your extra special wound
a warrant to judge my tired hands in honor of your plague
Forgive me it's easy to blame everyone except myself
I didn't think god could be this cruel
But strong evidence suggests otherwise. please Forgive me
if i say healthy childhoods are still and sigh like a lake
The father remembers every birthday and favorite color
I've never seen a lake, i will never know
how it feels to be complete
i grew up by the beach and When father breaks my voice i flood
i will never know how it feels to be complete. today
I want to throw stones with each ache
inside the happy childhoods of others, Mapping
where they land i try to imagine a cemented feeling of security.
unsalted, lakes do feel the weight of stones
i will never know how it feels to be complete
she called to describe how my hollow saturates her air
she glares into a mirror when she speaks
when she feels. Her reflections can't be everywhere
but she wants them to be everywhere there is nowhere
to console her. I am not you. we cannot ever be consoled.
I am not you. Get your hands off my broken heart. I am not

you. as if it were your own, there is nowhere
to console her. I grieve and grieve and yes
my parents are still alive.
I grieve and she still sees someone else
every time she looks at me.
I grieve and No, no one has my permission.
I have enough trouble starting my days as is stop. With you.stop.
looking over my shoulder stop because i cannot trust you stop
because I also cannot trust myself stop
your award winning crying, stop your stubborn showcase of
your beginning and your end. stop
You fall doubting my reflection stop i will never be enough
to soothe you stop I love you so much
why can't you see that
You've hurt me so much

I Am Not a Waterside Nymph

I know why you are better than me
you know that I am fiction
that I have not been paid
seen, heard, or understood

Niagara Falls Falls Falls

okay you play yourself
a pile of glass slippers
big budget expression
magic hour on the beach

Driving Lessons

We held down the car horn to shut you up
You can hardly hear a thing
Inside Closets
Beneath bed frames

this is normal
So i won't be able to acknowledge my fear
Or your Screaming

shattered glass, Secret bruising
Run away from home
The rules of this game are simple
you go deaf you win

You Will Be Beautiful to Look At

a girl pees between two cars that are parallel parked
yet you are the one who disgusts her
she is laughing at you while you hold your phone to record her

I Know Whoever Sees Me Dance Is Gonna Like It

I know that I can use you at least
if I see you, but for those who cannot sell or produce
whose dysfunction does not even exist as waste

in this world. who knows the master wasted object

I know objectification is a totalitarian function
I know that i too am a product
and perhaps that i have belonged to you

for all of us have been in the marketing business, we know
to sleep with golden rules and how natural has this gold
become: "if that product's no good just throw it out"

Very Exciting New Service

Discover a new reflection within the conditioned performance we may or may not have been subjected to. Mediate yourself through me. I, Google consciousness. I, the masturbation ceremony with the knife. I, the back door, the time of protein. Aliquam tempus convallis.

'the saddle on the horse'

Intimacy is far more abandoned with the distance and absence of physical presence. I want to lie down with you in virtual coitus. Your hunger will be exhibited but your insecurities will continue to be maintained by the anxiety sector of your private organism. Nam volutpat imperdiet sollicitudin.

'no touching'

Look outside the window. Now you are the one managing the emotional states of the consumer, my own feelings, or whatever being of the network; the act of self-exposure lies within itself. You can be the recipient of either.

'how awesome' I was calling my own name

Fuck me gently with a chainsaw. Customize your whatever. Exalt the desire instinct that makes us human. Nulla non tellus pharetra gravida. Integers are the ultimate corpse. The cloud in your head is also in my bed.

'wasteland is me'

Farther Father, Farther

congruent
to
my
fears

my
manners
are
impeccable

3.42 Seconds of I Didn't Fear Death Didn't Fear Life

we did have some fun
we died / have some fun

Things We Cannot Read or Say

Ceramic candles
my parents' love
Pay me
With your delicate wick
as I watch videos of my childhood
and death playback on loop

I Want the Truth Like an Asymptote Wants Zero

I'd like to spare you the paranoid math, the patterns
that perform like controlled demolitions
so please stand back and watch the ghost of our building undress
its debris will fall on you like cloud nine and electroshock

Personal Inscription

'this belongs to me' or
'this came from here'
the body

upon which
you left your signature
the good prison

once written
you opened me up
like a book

NOTES ON *GOODNIGHT SWEET THING*

Girls Gone Wild (Spring Break) appeared in *The Whitney Review of New Writing* Issue 2.

Being Hot and Poor Is Sad, *Mouth-To-Mouth Resuscitation*, and *Goodnight Sweet Thing* appeared in *Total Pet* Volume 3.

God Is the Space Between You and Me appeared in *Forever Magazine* Issue 3.

Last Night I Felt Afraid to Die appeared in *Softee Zine*.

Oh, to Give Myself to a Black Hole, *Extinction Level Event (Ask Your Parents)*, and *Feudal Mutations and Meditations* appeared in *Heavy Traffic*.

Extinction Level Event (Ask Your Parents) appeared in *The Drunken Canal* Issue 8.

Lazy Captive Saturday, *Mouth-To-Mouth Resuscitation*, and *Goodnight Sweet Thing* appeared in *Animal Blood* Issue 5.

NOTES ON *POEMS*

Poems (2008-2018) was originally published by Codétte.

Block of Tongue appeared in *Publishing Genius*.

Very Exciting New Service appeared in *Fanzine*.

China Video Diary, *Sofia*, *Images for Bad Acting*, and *Do Your Chores* appeared in *New York Tyrant*.

Safe Words and *You Can't Wear Chanel to Your Own Systematic Humiliation* appeared in *Apogee*.

How Much Do You Charge for Your Dignity?, *I'm Ready for My Clothes Off*, *Hi Girls Sleep Outside*, and *Dear Warden* appeared in *Gemstone Readings*.

Queen for a Day, *What You Have Inside Is What You Have to Sell*, and *In Nature* appeared in *Tagvverk*.

Cheating Eyes, the Video appeared in *E Ratio Postmodern Poetry Journal*.

Mother Superior Joan of the Angels and *Five Things Never to Touch* appeared in *How to Sleep Faster* Issue 6.

Personal Inscription, *Differentiate Me From a Doormat*, *Happy Birthday*, and *You Will Be Beautiful to Look At* appeared in *Codétte* Issue 1.

ACKNOWLEDGEMENTS

Thank you Brad Phillips.

Thank you Joseph Ian Henrikson, Ben Fama, Allie Rowbottom, Olivia West Lloyd, Sigrid Lauren, Manon Lutanie, Yancey Strickler, Gina Pham, K.O. Namidie, Tasneem Sarkez, Patricia Margarita Hernandez, Lora Nouk, Jon Lindsey, and Steph Kretowicz.

ABOUT THE AUTHOR

Cristine Brache is an artist and filmmaker living and working in New York. She received her MFA in Fine Art Media from the Slade School of Fine Art (London, UK). Her debut poetry collection, entitled *Poems*, was published in 2018 by Codétte. Her work has been exhibited internationally at galleries and institutions like Berlinische Galerie and ICA Miami and critically reviewed in places such as *The New York Times*, *Artforum*, *The New Yorker*, and *The Los Angeles Review of Books*.